ASSORTED ROUTINES FOR VB.NET

Code you need

Richard Thomas Edwards

CONTENTS

Let's dive right in

You never know what you are missing until you can't find it.
—*Richard Thomas Edwards*

I have no reason for writing this book other than wanting to share with you some routines I have collected over the years that were necessary to test and trouble shoot connectivity between machines.

With that said, all of the code here is part of a single module that you can use as a single module or parts that you want to use can be pulled out and worked with as a single function.

Below is, essentially, the initialization code:

```
Imports Microsoft.Win32
Imports WSManAutomation
Imports System.Diagnostics
Imports System.DirectoryServices

Module Module1

    Public txtstream As Object

    Public ipdic As Object = CreateObject("Scripting.Dictionary")
```

Public Declare Ansi Function ShellExecute Lib "shell32.dll" Alias "ShellExecuteA" (ByVal hwnd As Integer, ByVal lpOperation As String, ByVal lpFile As String, ByVal lpParameters As String, ByVal lpDirectory As String, ByVal nShowCmd As Integer) As Integer

Public Declare Ansi Function WNetConnectionDialog Lib "mpr.dll" Alias "WNetConnectionDialog" (ByVal hwnd As Integer, ByVal dwType As Integer) As Integer

Public Declare Ansi Function WNetDisconnectDialog Lib "mpr.dll" Alias "WNetDisconnectDialog" (ByVal hwnd As Integer, ByVal dwType As Integer) As Integer


```
Const NET_FW_IP_VERSION_V4 = 0
Const NET_FW_IP_VERSION_V6 = 1
Const NET_FW_IP_VERSION_ANY = 2

Const NET_FW_IP_PROTOCOL_UDP = 17
Const NET_FW_IP_PROTOCOL_TCP = 6

Const NET_FW_SCOPE_ALL = 0
Const NET_FW_SCOPE_LOCAL_SUBNET = 1

Dim Allowed
 Dim Restricted
```

ADSI Code
Performing a computer look up

```vb
        Public  Function  Perform_ADSIComputerLookup(ByVal  DN  As  String)  As
String


    Try

        Dim  Domain  As  Object  =  GetObject("WinNT://"  &  DN  &  "/"  &
System.Environment.MachineName & ", computer")
        Return Domain

    Catch ex As Exception

    End Try

    Return ""

End Function

Public Function Test_Well_Known_Port() As String


    Application.DoEvents()
    Dim fwMgr As Object
    Try
        Dim ip As String = ipdic(System.Environment.MachineName)
        fwMgr = CreateObject("HNetCfg.FwMgr", ip)
```

```vb
                fwMgr.IsPortAllowed(vbNullString, NET_FW_IP_VERSION_V4, 7, ip,
NET_FW_IP_PROTOCOL_TCP, Allowed, Restricted)
                Return System.Environment.MachineName & " port 7 allowed =" &
Allowed & ", Restricted = " & Restricted


        Catch ex As Exception

                Return (System.Environment.MachineName & " threw exception " &
ex.Message)


        End Try

        fwMgr = Nothing


    End Function
```

Testing Local 32-bit registry connectivity

```
Public Function Test_Open_32Bit_Registry() As String

    Try

        Dim        regkey        As        RegistryKey        =
RegistryKey.OpenBaseKey(RegistryHive.LocalMachine, RegistryView.Registry32)
        Return   System.Environment.MachineName   &   " Remote  registry
connectivity = Success"

    Catch ex As Exception

    End Try

    Return ""


End Function
```

Testing Local 64-bit registry connectivity

```
Public Function Test_Open_64Bit_Registry() As String

    Try

        Dim          regkey          As          RegistryKey          =
RegistryKey.OpenRemoteBaseKey(RegistryHive.LocalMachine,
RegistryView.Registry64)
        Return    System.Environment.MachineName    &    " Remote  registry
connectivity = Success"

    Catch ex As Exception

    End Try

    Return ""

End Function
```

Testing Remote 32-bit registry connectivity

Public Function **Test_Open_Remote_32Bit_Registry()** As String

```
        Try

            Dim        regkey        As        RegistryKey        =
RegistryKey.OpenRemoteBaseKey(RegistryHive.LocalMachine,
System.Environment.MachineName, RegistryView.Registry32)
            Return   System.Environment.MachineName   &   " Remote  registry
connectivity = Success"

        Catch ex As Exception

        End Try

        Return ""

        End Function
```

Testing Remote 64-bit registry connectivity

```vb
Public Function Test_Open_64Bit_Remote_Registry() As String

    Try

        Dim regkey As RegistryKey = RegistryKey.OpenRemoteBaseKey(RegistryHive.LocalMachine, System.Environment.MachineName, RegistryView.Registry64)
        Return System.Environment.MachineName & " Remote registry connectivity = Success"

    Catch ex As Exception

    End Try

    Return System.Environment.MachineName & " Remote registry connectivity = Failed"

End Function
```

Testing Remote Event Log connectivity

```
Public Function Test_RemoteEventLogTest(ByVal RMachine As String) As
Boolean

    Try
        Dim et() As EventLog = EventLog.GetEventLogs(RMachine)
        Return System.Environment.MachineName & " EventLog Access =
succeeded"

    Catch ex As Exception

    End Try

    Return System.Environment.MachineName & " EventLog Access = failed"

End Function
```

Testing Remote File connectivity

```vbnet
Public Function Test_RemoteFSOConnectivity(ByVal ComputerName As String) As String

    Application.DoEvents()
    Dim fso As Object = CreateObject("Scripting.FileSystemObject", ComputerName)
    Try

        Return ComputerName & " Remote FileSystemObject = succeeded"

    Catch ex As Exception

        Return ComputerName & " threw exception " & ex.Message

    End Try

End Function
```

System Environment Functions

Get Computer Name

```
Public Function Get_Computer_Name() As String

    Return System.Environment.MachineName

End Function
```

Get User Name

```
Public Function Get_User_Name() As String

    Return System.Environment.UserName

End Function
```

Get Domain Name

```
Public Function Get_Domain_Name() As String

    Return System.Environment.UserDomainName

End Function
```

Getting the IP Address

```vb
Public Function Get_IP_Address(ByVal hostname As String) As String

    Dim al() As System.Net.IPAddress = System.Net.Dns.GetHostEntry(hostname).AddressList
    For Each ip As System.Net.IPAddress In al
        'Only return IPv4 routable IPs
        If (ip.AddressFamily = System.Net.Sockets.AddressFamily.InterNetwork) Then
            Dim pos As Integer = InStr(ip.ToString, ".")
            If pos <> 0 Then
                If pos < 5 Then
                    Dim tempstr As String = ip.ToString()
                    Return ip.ToString
                    Exit For
                End If
            End If
        End If
    Next

    Return ""

End Function
```

Ping Remote Computer

```vbnet
Public Function Test_Ping(ByVal hostname As String) As Boolean

    Dim objs = GetObject("Winmgmts:\\.\root\cimv2").ExecQuery("Select *
From Win32_PingStatus where Address='" & hostname & "'")
    For Each obj In objs
      If obj.Statuscode = 0 Then
        Return True
        Exit Function
      Else
        Return GetStatusCode(obj.StatusCode)
        Exit Function
    Next


End Function

Function GetStatusCode(ByVal intCode) As String

    Dim strStatus

    Select Case intCode
      Case 0
        strStatus = "Success"
      Case 11001
        strStatus = "Buffer Too Small"
      Case 11002
        strStatus = "Destination Net Unreachable"
      Case 11003
        strStatus = "Destination Host Unreachable"
      Case 11004
        strStatus = "Destination Protocol Unreachable"
      Case 11005
        strStatus = "Destination Port Unreachable"
```

```
    Case 11006
       strStatus = "No Resources"
    Case 11007
       strStatus = "Bad Option"
    Case 11008
       strStatus = "Hardware Error"
    Case 11009
       strStatus = "Packet Too Big"
    Case 11010
       strStatus = "Request Timed Out"
    Case 11011
       strStatus = "Bad Request"
    Case 11012
       strStatus = "Bad Route"
    Case 11013
       strStatus = "TimeToLive Expired Transit"
    Case 11014
       strStatus = "TimeToLive Expired Reassembly"
    Case 11015
       strStatus = "Parameter Problem"
    Case 11016
       strStatus = "Source Quench"
    Case 11017
       strStatus = "Option Too Big"
    Case 11018
       strStatus = "Bad Destination"
    Case 11032
       strStatus = "Negotiating IPSEC"
    Case 11050
       strStatus = "General Failure"
    Case Else
       strStatus = intCode & " - Unknown"
  End Select
  GetStatusCode = strStatus

End Function
```

Ping From Remote Computer

```vb
        Public Function Test_Ping(ByVal hostname As String, ByVal ReturnName As
String) As Boolean

        Dim svc As Object = GetObject("winmgmts:\\" & hostname &
"\root\cimv2")
        Dim objs As Object = svc.ExecQuery("Select * from Win32_PingStatus", ,
48)
        For Each obj In objs
            Try

                Return obj.Properties_.Item(ReturnName).Value.ToString

            Catch ex As Exception

                Return GetStatusCode(obj.StatusCode)

            End Try

        Next

        Return ""

    End Function




    Function GetStatusCode(ByVal intCode) As String

        Dim strStatus

        Select Case intCode
            Case 0
```

```
    strStatus = "Success"
Case 11001
    strStatus = "Buffer Too Small"
Case 11002
    strStatus = "Destination Net Unreachable"
Case 11003
    strStatus = "Destination Host Unreachable"
Case 11004
    strStatus = "Destination Protocol Unreachable"
Case 11005
    strStatus = "Destination Port Unreachable"
Case 11006
    strStatus = "No Resources"
Case 11007
    strStatus = "Bad Option"
Case 11008
    strStatus = "Hardware Error"
Case 11009
    strStatus = "Packet Too Big"
Case 11010
    strStatus = "Request Timed Out"
Case 11011
    strStatus = "Bad Request"
Case 11012
    strStatus = "Bad Route"
Case 11013
    strStatus = "TimeToLive Expired Transit"
Case 11014
    strStatus = "TimeToLive Expired Reassembly"
Case 11015
    strStatus = "Parameter Problem"
Case 11016
    strStatus = "Source Quench"
Case 11017
    strStatus = "Option Too Big"
Case 11018
    strStatus = "Bad Destination"
Case 11032
    strStatus = "Negotiating IPSEC"
Case 11050
```

```
            strStatus = "General Failure"
        Case Else
            strStatus = intCode & " - Unknown"
    End Select
    GetStatusCode = strStatus

End Function
```

Test Local WMI Connectivity

```vb
Public Function Test_Local_WMI(ByVal AuthenticationLevel As String,
ByVal ImpersonationLevel As String, ByVal ns As String, ByVal classname As String)
As Boolean

    Try

        Dim svc As Object = GetObject("winmgmts:\\.\" & ns)
        svc.Security_.AuthenticationLevel = AuthenticationLevel
        svc.Security_.ImpersonationLevel = ImpersonationLevel
        Dim objs As Object = svc.InstancesOf(classname)

        For Each obj As Object In objs
            Exit For
        Next

        Return True

    Catch ex As Exception

        Return False

    End Try


End Function
```

Test Remote WMI Connectivity

```vb
Public Function Test_Remote_WMI(ByVal ComputerName As String, ByVal
UserName As String, ByVal Password As String, ByVal AuthenticationLevel As String,
ByVal ImpersonationLevel As String, ByVal ns As String, ByVal classname As String)
As Boolean


        Try

                Dim l As Object = CreateObject("Wbemscripting.SWbemLocator")
                Dim svc As Object = l.connectserver(ComputerName, ns, UserName,
Password)
                svc.Security_.AuthenticationLevel = AuthenticationLevel
                svc.Security_.ImpersonationLevel = ImpersonationLevel
                Dim objs As Object = svc.InstancesOf(classname)

                For Each obj As Object In objs
                   Exit For
                Next

                Return True

        Catch ex As Exception

                Return False
```

Test WinRM Connectivity

```vb
Public Function Test_WinRM(ByVal URL As String, ByVal ns As String, ByVal
Classname As String) As Boolean

    Try

        Dim strDialect As String =
"http://schemas.microsoft.com/wbem/wsman/1/WQL"
        Dim strResource As Object =
"http://schemas.microsoft.com/wbem/wsman/1/wmi/" & ns
        Dim objWsman As WSMan = New WSMan
        Dim objSession As IWSManSession = objWsman.CreateSession(URL)
        Dim strFilter As String = "SELECT * FROM " & Classname
        Dim objResultSet As Object = objSession.Enumerate(strResource,
strFilter, strDialect)

        Return True

    Catch ex As Exception

        Debug.Print(ex.Message)

        Return False

    End Try
```

End Function

Get Local Computer OS Architecture

```
Public Function Get_OS_Architecture() As String

    Dim l As Object = CreateObject("Wbemscripting.SWbemLocator")
    Dim svc As Object = l.connectserver(".", "root\cimv2")
    svc.Security_.AuthenticationLevel = 6
    svc.Security_.ImpersonationLevel = 3
    Dim objs As Object = svc.InstancesOf("Win32_OperatingSystem")

    For Each obj In objs

      Try
        Return obj.OSArchitecture

      Catch ex As Exception
        Return ""
      End Try
```

```
Next

    Return ""

End Function
```

Get Local Address Width

```vb
Public Function Get_Address_Width() As String

    Dim l As Object = CreateObject("Wbemscripting.SWbemLocator")
    Dim svc As Object = l.connectserver(".", "root\cimv2")
    svc.Security_.AuthenticationLevel = 6
    svc.Security_.ImpersonationLevel = 3
    Dim objs As Object = svc.InstancesOf("Win32_Processor")

    For Each obj In objs

        Try
            Return obj.AddressWidth

        Catch ex As Exception
            Return ""
        End Try

    Next

    Return ""

End Function
```

Get OS Version

```
Public Function Get_OSVersion() As String

    Dim l As Object = CreateObject("Wbemscripting.SWbemLocator")
    Dim svc As Object = l.connectserver(".", "root\cimv2")
    svc.Security_.AuthenticationLevel = 6
    svc.Security_.ImpersonationLevel = 3
    Dim objs As Object = svc.InstancesOf("Win32_OperatinSystem")

    For Each obj In objs

        Try

            Return obj.OSVersion

        Catch ex As Exception
            Return ""
        End Try

    Next

    Return ""

End Function
```

Get BIOS Version

```vb
Public Function Get_BIOS_Version() As String

    Dim l As Object = CreateObject("Wbemscripting.SWbemLocator")
    Dim svc As Object = l.connectserver(".", "root\cimv2")
    svc.Security_.AuthenticationLevel = 6
    svc.Security_.ImpersonationLevel = 3
    Dim objs As Object = svc.InstancesOf("Win32_BIOS")

    For Each obj In objs

        Try

            Return obj.Version

        Catch ex As Exception
            Return ""
        End Try

    Next

    Return ""

End Function
```

Get Desktop ICONS

```vb
Public Function Get_Desktop_Icons() As String()

    Dim ws As Object = CreateObject("WScript.Shell")
    Dim desktop As String = ws.SpecialFolders("Desktop")
    Dim names() As String = Nothing
    Dim x As Integer = 0

    Dim fso As Object = CreateObject("Scripting.FileSystemObject")
    Dim fldr As Object = fso.GetFolder(desktop)
    For Each file As Object In fldr.Files
        Dim pos As Integer = InStr(file.Name, ".lnk")
        If pos Then
            ReDim Preserve names(x + 1)
            names(x) = file.Name
        End If
    Next

    If names.GetLength(0) <> 0 Then
        Return names
    End If

    Return names

End Function
```

Create Desktop Icons

```
        Public   Sub   Create_Desktop_Icons(ByVal   FullPath   As   String,   ByVal
ShortcutName As String, ByVal Description As String, ByVal IconLocation As String,
ByVal hotkey As String)

        Dim ws As Object = CreateObject("WScript.Shell")
        Dim strdt As String = ws.SpecialFolders("Desktop")
        Dim oLink As Object = ws.CreateShortcut(strdt & "\" & ShortcutName &
".lnk")
        oLink.TargetPath = FullPath
        oLink.WindowStyle = 1
        If hotkey <> "" Then
           oLink.Hotkey = hotkey
        End If

        If IconLocation <> "" Then
           oLink.IconLocation = IconLocation
        End If
        oLink.Description = Description
        oLink.WorkingDirectory = strdt
        oLink.Save()

    End Sub
```

Enumerate Through Desktop Short Cuts

```vb
Public Function Enumerate_Through_Desktop_ShortCuts(ByVal FullPath As
String, ByVal ShortcutName As String) As String()

    Dim ws As Object = CreateObject("WScript.Shell")
    Dim strdt As String = ws.SpecialFolders("Desktop")

    Dim names() As String = Nothing
    Dim x As Integer = 0

    Dim fso As Object = CreateObject("Scripting.FileSystemObject")
    Dim fldr As Object = fso.GetFolder(strdt)
    For Each file As Object In fldr.Files
        Dim pos As Integer = InStr(file.Name, ".lnk")
        If pos Then
            ReDim Preserve names(x + 1)
            names(x) = file.Name
        End If
    Next
    If names.GetLength(0) <> 0 Then
        Return names
    End If
End Function
```

Delete Desktop Icon

```vbnet
Public Sub Delete_Desktop_Icon(ByVal killfile As String)

    Dim ws As Object = CreateObject("WScript.Shell")
    Dim strdt As String = ws.SpecialFolders("Desktop")

    Dim names() As String = Nothing
    Dim x As Integer = 0

    Dim fso As Object = CreateObject("Scripting.FileSystemObject")
    Dim fldr As Object = fso.GetFolder(strdt)
    For Each file As Object In fldr.Files
        Dim pos As Integer = InStr(file.Name, killfile)
        If pos Then
            fso.DeleteFile(file.path)
        End If
    Next

End Sub
```

Create Desktop Web Link

```vb
Public Sub Create_Desktop_Web_Link(ByVal FullPath As String, ByVal ShortcutName As String)

    Dim ws As Object = CreateObject("WScript.Shell")
    Dim strdt As String = ws.SpecialFolders("Desktop")
    Dim oLink As Object = ws.CreateShortcut(strdt & "\" & ShortcutName & ".url")
    oLink.TargetPath = FullPath
    oLink.Save()

End Sub
```

Enumerate Through Desktop Web Links

```vb
Public    Function    Enumerate_Through_Web_Desktop_Web_Link(ByVal
FullPath As String, ByVal ShortcutName As String) As String()

    Dim ws As Object = CreateObject("WScript.Shell")
    Dim strdt As String = ws.SpecialFolders("Desktop")

    Dim names() As String = Nothing
    Dim x As Integer = 0

    Dim fso As Object = CreateObject("Scripting.FileSystemObject")
    Dim fldr As Object = fso.GetFolder(strdt)
    For Each file As Object In fldr.Files
        Dim pos As Integer = InStr(file.Name, ".url")
        If pos Then
            ReDim Preserve names(x + 1)
            names(x) = file.Name
        End If
    Next

    If names.GetLength(0) <> 0 Then
        Return names
    End If

    Return names

End Function
```

Delete Desktop Web Link

```
Public Sub Delete_Desktop_Web_Link(ByVal killfile As String)

    Dim ws As Object = CreateObject("WScript.Shell")
    Dim strdt As String = ws.SpecialFolders("Desktop")

    Dim names() As String = Nothing
    Dim x As Integer = 0

    Dim fso As Object = CreateObject("Scripting.FileSystemObject")
    Dim fldr As Object = fso.GetFolder(strdt)
    For Each file As Object In fldr.Files
        Dim pos As Integer = InStr(file.Name, killfile)
        If pos Then
            fso.DeleteFile(file.path)
        End If
    Next

End Sub
```

Get List Of Running Processes

```
Public Function Get_List_Of_Runing_Processes() As String()


    Dim l As Object = CreateObject("Wbemscripting.SWbemLocator")
    Dim svc As Object = l.connectserver(".", "root\cimv2")
    svc.Security_.AuthenticationLevel = 6
    svc.Security_.ImpersonationLevel = 3
    Dim objs As Object = svc.InstancesOf("Win32_Process")

    Dim names() As String = Nothing
    Dim x As Integer = 0

    For Each obj In objs
       ReDim Preserve names(x + 1)
       names(x) = obj.Name
       x = x + 1
    Next

    Return names

End Function
```

Get List Of Running Services

```
Public Function Get_List_Of_Runing_Services() As String()


    Dim l As Object = CreateObject("Wbemscripting.SWbemLocator")
    Dim svc As Object = l.connectserver(".", "root\cimv2")
    svc.Security_.AuthenticationLevel = 6
    svc.Security_.ImpersonationLevel = 3
    Dim objs As Object = svc.InstancesOf("Win32_Service")

    Dim names() As String = Nothing
    Dim x As Integer = 0

    For Each obj In objs
        ReDim Preserve names(x + 1)
        names(x) = obj.Name
        x = x + 1
    Next

    Return names

End Function
```

Discover Pending Restart

```vb
Public Function Discover_Pending_Restart() As Boolean

    Dim Su As Integer = 0
    Dim Fa As Integer = 0
    Dim er As Integer = 0

    Const HKEY_LOCAL_MACHINE = &H80000002


    Try

        Dim svc As Object = GetObject("Winmgmts:\\.\root\cimv2")
        svc.Security_.AuthenticationLevel = 6
        svc.Security_.ImpersonationLevel = 3

        Dim oReg As Object = svc.Get("StdRegProv")

        Dim          strKeyPath          As          String          =
"SYSTEM\CurrentControlSet\Control\Session Manager"
        Dim vn() As Object = Nothing
        Dim vt() As Object = Nothing
        Dim iret As Integer = oReg.enumvalues(HKEY_LOCAL_MACHINE,
strKeyPath, vn, vt)
            If iret = 0 Then
                For Each v In vn
                    Dim pos As Integer = InStr(v, "Pending")
                    If pos > 0 Then
                        Return True
```

```
                End If
            Next
        End If


    Catch ex As Exception

    End Try

    Return False

End Function
```

Enumerate Registry Keys

```vb
Public Sub EnumKeys(ByVal oreg As Object, ByVal HKEY_LOCAL_MACHINE
As Integer, ByVal Path As String)

    txtstream.WriteLine(Path)
    EnumValues(oreg, HKEY_LOCAL_MACHINE, Path)

    Dim arrSubKeys = Nothing
    Try

        Dim iret As Integer = oreg.EnumKey(HKEY_LOCAL_MACHINE, Path,
arrSubKeys)

        If IsDBNull(arrSubKeys) = False Then
            For v As Integer = 0 To UBound(arrSubKeys) - 1
                EnumKeys(oreg,    HKEY_LOCAL_MACHINE,    Path    &    "\"    &
arrSubKeys(v))
            Next
        End If

    Catch ex As Exception

    End Try


End Sub
```

Enumerate Registry Values

```vb
Public    Sub    EnumValues(ByVal    oreg    As    Object,    ByVal
HKEY_LOCAL_MACHINE As Integer, ByVal Path As String)


    Const REG_SZ = 1
    Const REG_EXPAND_SZ = 2
    Const REG_BINARY = 3
    Const REG_DWORD = 4
    Const REG_MULTI_SZ = 7

    Dim iret As Integer

    Dim vn() As Object = Nothing
    Dim vt() As Object = Nothing

    iret = oreg.enumvalues(HKEY_LOCAL_MACHINE, Path, vn, vt)
    If IsNothing(vn) = True Then
        Exit Sub
    Else
        If IsDBNull(vn) = True Then
            Exit Sub
        Else

            For v As Integer = 0 To vn.GetLength(0) - 1

                Dim Name As String = ""
                Dim dt As String = ""
                Dim value As Object = Nothing

                Name = vn(v)

                Select Case vt(v)

                    Case REG_SZ
```

```vb
            dt = "REG_SZ"

            iret = oreg.GetStringValue(HKEY_LOCAL_MACHINE, Path,
Name, value)

        Case REG_EXPAND_SZ

            dt = "REG_EXPAND_SZ"

            iret = oreg.GetExpandedStringValue(HKEY_LOCAL_MACHINE,
Path, Name, value)

        Case REG_BINARY

            dt = "REG_BINARY"

            Dim strValue() As String = Nothing

            iret = oreg.GetBinaryValue(HKEY_LOCAL_MACHINE, Path,
Name, strValue)

            For j = LBound(strValue) To UBound(strValue)
              If value <> "" Then
                value = value & ", "
              End If
              Dim myhex As String = ""
              If Len(Hex(CInt(strValue(j)))) = 1 Then
                myhex = "0" & Hex(CInt(strValue(j)))
              Else
                myhex = Hex(CInt(strValue(j)))
              End If

              value = value + myhex
            Next

        Case REG_DWORD

            dt = "REG_DWORD"
            Dim dwValue As Integer
```

```vb
                    iret  =  oreg.GetDwordValue(HKEY_LOCAL_MACHINE,  Path,
Name, dwValue)
                    value = dwValue.ToString

            Case REG_MULTI_SZ

              dt = "REG_MULTI_SZ"

              Dim vls As Object = Nothing
              Dim Ve As Object = Nothing
              oreg.GetMultiStringValue(HKEY_LOCAL_MACHINE,        Path,
Name, vls)
              Dim vl As Object
              For Each vl In vls
                If Ve <> "" Then
                  Ve = Ve & ", "
                End If
                Ve = Ve + vl
              Next
              value = Ve.ToString()
            End Select

          If Trim(vn(v)) = "" Then
            Name = "(Default)"
          Else
            Name = vn(v)
          End If

          txtstream.WriteLine(Name & "," & dt & "," & value)

        Next

      End If

    End If

  End Sub
```

Reset FireWall

```vb
Public Function Reset_Firewall(ByVal ComputerName As String) As Boolean

    Try
        Dim Process As New Process
        Dim info As New ProcessStartInfo
        info.WindowStyle = ProcessWindowStyle.Hidden
        info.FileName = "cmd.exe"
        info.Arguments = "/c netsh firewall reset"
        Process.Start(info)

        Return True

    Catch ex As Exception

        Return False

    End Try

End Function
```

Reset NIC

```vbnet
Public Function Reset_Nic(ByVal ComputerName As String) As Boolean

    Try

        Dim Process As New Process
        Dim info As New ProcessStartInfo
        info.WindowStyle = ProcessWindowStyle.Hidden
        info.FileName = "cmd.exe"
        info.Arguments = "/c netsh winsock reset"
        Process.Start(info)

        Return True

    Catch ex As Exception

        Return False

    End Try

End Function
```

Reset NIC Catalog

```vb
Public Function Reset_Nic_Catalog(ByVal ComputerName As String) As Boolean

    Try

        Dim Process As New Process
        Dim info As New ProcessStartInfo
        info.WindowStyle = ProcessWindowStyle.Hidden
        info.FileName = "cmd.exe"
        info.Arguments = "/c netsh winsock reset catalog"
        Process.Start(info)

        Return True

    Catch ex As Exception

        Return False

    End Try

End Function
```

Pin To Taskbar

```
Public Sub Pin_To_Taskbar()

    Dim ShellApp, FSO, Desktop
    ShellApp = CreateObject("Shell.Application")
    FSO = CreateObject("Scripting.FileSystemObject")

    Desktop = ShellApp.NameSpace("C:\Users\Wayne\Desktop")

    Dim LnkFile
    LnkFile = Desktop.Self.Path & "\ScheduleNotifier.lnk"

    If (FSO.FileExists(LnkFile)) Then
        Dim tmp As String = ""
        Dim verb As Object = Nothing
        For Each verb In Desktop.ParseName("ScheduleNotifier.lnk").Verbs
            tmp = tmp & verb & Chr(13)
        Next
        MsgBox(tmp)

        Dim desktopImtes, item
        desktopImtes = Desktop.Items()

        For Each item In desktopImtes
            If (item.Name = "ScheduleNotifier") Then
                'MsgBox(item.Name)
                For Each verb In item.Verbs
                    If (verb.Name = "Pin to Tas&kbar") Then
                        verb.DoIt()
                    End If
```

```vb
            Next
        End If
    Next

    End If

    FSO = Nothing
    ShellApp = Nothing

End Sub
```

Unpin From Taskbar

```vbnet
Public Sub unPin_TaskBar()

    Dim ShellApp, FSO, Desktop
    ShellApp = CreateObject("Shell.Application")
    FSO = CreateObject("Scripting.FileSystemObject")

    Desktop = ShellApp.NameSpace("C:\Users\Wayne\Desktop")

    Dim LnkFile
    LnkFile = Desktop.Self.Path & "\ScheduleNotifier.lnk"

    If (FSO.FileExists(LnkFile)) Then
        Dim tmp As String = ""
        Dim verb As Object = Nothing
        For Each verb In Desktop.ParseName("ScheduleNotifier.lnk").Verbs
            tmp = tmp & verb & Chr(13)
        Next
        MsgBox(tmp)

        Dim desktopImtes, item
        desktopImtes = Desktop.Items()

        For Each item In desktopImtes
            If (item.Name = "ScheduleNotifier") Then
                'MsgBox(item.Name)
                For Each verb In item.Verbs
                    If (verb.Name = "Unpin from Tas&kbar") _
    Then 'If (verb.Name = "从任务栏脱离(&K)")
                        verb.DoIt()
                    End If
                Next
            End If
        End If
```

```vba
        Next

    End If

    FSO = Nothing
    ShellApp = Nothing
End Sub
```

Delete Folder Files and Sub Folders

```vbnet
Private Function deleteFolderFilesAndSubFolders(ByVal location As System.IO.DirectoryInfo, Optional ByVal exclude As String = "") As Boolean

    Try

        For Each f As System.IO.DirectoryInfo In location.GetDirectories
            For Each i As System.IO.FileInfo In f.GetFiles
                i.Delete()
            Next
            f.Delete()
        Next

        Return True

    Catch ex As Exception

        Return False

    End Try


End Function
```

Get Value Routine

```
Public Function GetValue(ByVal name, ByVal obj)

    Dim pos
    Dim tempstr
    Dim tName
    tempstr = obj.GetObjectText_
    tName = name & " = "
    pos = InStr(tempstr, tName)
    If pos Then
        pos = pos + Len(name & " = ")
        tempstr = Mid(tempstr, pos, Len(tempstr))
        pos = InStr(tempstr, ";")
        tempstr = Mid(tempstr, 1, pos - 1)
        tempstr = Replace(tempstr, Chr(34), "")
        tempstr = Replace(tempstr, "{", "")
        tempstr = Replace(tempstr, "}", "")
        If Len(tempstr) > 13 And obj.Properties_(name).CIMType = 101 Then
            tempstr = Mid(tempstr, 5, 2) & "/" & _
                    Mid(tempstr, 7, 2) & "/" & _
                    Mid(tempstr, 1, 4) & " " & _
                    Mid(tempstr, 9, 2) & ":" & _
                    Mid(tempstr, 11, 2) & ":" & _
                    Mid(tempstr, 13, 2)
        End If
        GetValue = tempstr
    Else
        GetValue = ""
    End If
End Function
```

Below, is a list of built in network functions

They are part of the System.Net.Networkinformation Namespace.
And I can safely say I haven't tried all of them out.

System.Net.NetworkInformation.DuplicateAddressDetectionState()
System.Net.NetworkInformation.GatewayIPAddressInformation()
System.Net.NetworkInformation.GatewayIPAddressInformationCollection()
System.Net.NetworkInformation.IcmpV4Statistics()
System.Net.NetworkInformation.IcmpV6Statistics()
System.Net.NetworkInformation.IPAddressCollection()
System.Net.NetworkInformation.IPAddressInformation()
System.Net.NetworkInformation.IPAddressInformationCollection()
System.Net.NetworkInformation.IPGlobalProperties()
System.Net.NetworkInformation.IPGlobalStatistics()
System.Net.NetworkInformation.IPInterfaceProperties()
System.Net.NetworkInformation.IPv4InterfaceStatistics()
System.Net.NetworkInformation.IPv6InterfaceProperties()
System.Net.NetworkInformation.MulticastIPAddressInformation()
System.Net.NetworkInformation.MulticastIPAddressInformationCollection()
System.Net.NetworkInformation.NetBiosNodeType()
System.Net.NetworkInformation.NetworkInterface()
System.Net.NetworkInformation.TcpConnectionInformation()
System.Net.NetworkInformation.TcpStatistics()
System.Net.NetworkInformation.UdpStatistics()
System.Net.NetworkInformation.UnicastIPAddressInformation()

The below code combines PowerShell with VB.Net,

```vbnet
Imports System.Management.Automation
Imports System.Management.Automation.Runspaces
Imports Microsoft.PowerShell.Cmdletization
Imports Microsoft.PowerShell.Commands
Imports Microsoft.PowerShell.Cim
Imports System.Runtime.Serialization

Public Class Form1

    Private Sub Form1_Load(sender As System.Object, e As
System.EventArgs) Handles MyBase.Load

    End Sub

    Private Sub ComboBox1_SelectedIndexChanged(sender As
System.Object, e As System.EventArgs) Handles
ComboBox1.SelectedIndexChanged
        If ComboBox1.Text = "*select An Option*" Then Exit Sub
        Dim txtstream As Object = Nothing
        Dim fso As Object =
CreateObject("Scripting.FileSystemObject")

        txtstream = fso.OpenTextFile(Application.StartupPath &
"\" & ComboBox1.Text & ".htm", 2, True, -2)
        txtstream.WriteLine("<html xmlns:v=""urn:schemas-
microsoft-com:vml"">")
        txtstream.WriteLine("<HEAD>")
        txtstream.WriteLine("<TITLE></TITLE>")
        txtstream.WriteLine("<STYLE type=text/css>")
        txtstream.WriteLine("v\:* { behavior: url(#default#VML);
}")
        txtstream.WriteLine("BODY {")
```

```
        txtstream.WriteLine("PADDING-RIGHT: 0px; PADDING-LEFT:
0px; PADDING-BOTTOM: 0px; FONT: 9pt Verdana,Arial,Helvetica;
COLOR: #ffffff; PADDING-TOP: 0px")
        txtstream.WriteLine("}")
        txtstream.WriteLine("TABLE {")
        txtstream.WriteLine("FONT: 9pt Verdana,Arial,Helvetica;
COLOR: antiquewhite; cursor:hand")
        txtstream.WriteLine("}")
        txtstream.WriteLine("TD {")
        txtstream.WriteLine("FONT: 9pt Verdana,Arial,Helvetica;
COLOR: #ffffff")
        txtstream.WriteLine("}")
        txtstream.WriteLine(".subjectbar {")
        txtstream.WriteLine("PADDING-RIGHT: 5px; PADDING-LEFT:
5px; FONT-WEIGHT: bold; FONT-SIZE: 11pt; PADDING-BOTTOM: 3px;
COLOR: #ffffff; PADDING-TOP: 3px; BACKGROUND-COLOR: #597fa1")
        txtstream.WriteLine("}")
        txtstream.WriteLine(".headingbar {")
        txtstream.WriteLine("PADDING-RIGHT: 5px; PADDING-LEFT:
5px; FONT-WEIGHT: bold; FONT-SIZE: 8pt; PADDING-BOTTOM: 3px;
COLOR: #ffffff; PADDING-TOP: 3px; BACKGROUND-COLOR: #114879")
        txtstream.WriteLine("}")
        txtstream.WriteLine(".navbar {")
        txtstream.WriteLine("PADDING-RIGHT: 5px; PADDING-LEFT:
5px; FONT-WEIGHT: bold; FONT-SIZE: 8px; PADDING-BOTTOM: 3px;
COLOR: #0d1826; PADDING-TOP: 3px; BACKGROUND-COLOR: #d4e1f1")
        txtstream.WriteLine("}")
        txtstream.WriteLine(".myclass")
        txtstream.WriteLine("{")
        txtstream.WriteLine("     BORDER-RIGHT: #999999 1px
solid;")
        txtstream.WriteLine("     PADDING-RIGHT: 1px;")
        txtstream.WriteLine("     PADDING-LEFT: 1px;")
        txtstream.WriteLine("     PADDING-BOTTOM: 1px;")
        txtstream.WriteLine("     LINE-HEIGHT: 14px;")
        txtstream.WriteLine("     PADDING-TOP: 1px;")
        txtstream.WriteLine("     BORDER-BOTTOM: #999 1px solid;")
        txtstream.WriteLine("     BACKGROUND-COLOR: #ffffff;")
        txtstream.WriteLine("
filter:progid:DXImageTransform.Microsoft.Shadow(color='navy',
Direction=135, Strength=32)")
        txtstream.WriteLine("}")
        txtstream.WriteLine(".myclass1")
        txtstream.WriteLine("{")
```

```
        txtstream.WriteLine("     BORDER-RIGHT: #999999 1px
solid;")
        txtstream.WriteLine("     PADDING-RIGHT: 3px;")
        txtstream.WriteLine("     PADDING-LEFT: 3px;")
        txtstream.WriteLine("     PADDING-BOTTOM: 3px;")
        txtstream.WriteLine("     LINE-HEIGHT: 12px;")
        txtstream.WriteLine("     PADDING-TOP: 1px;")
        txtstream.WriteLine("     BORDER-BOTTOM: #999 1px solid;")
        txtstream.WriteLine("     BACKGROUND-COLOR: #cccccc;")
        txtstream.WriteLine("
filter:progid:DXImageTransform.Microsoft.Shadow(color='black',
Direction=135, Strength=2)")
        txtstream.WriteLine("}")
        txtstream.WriteLine("</STYLE>")
        txtstream.WriteLine("")
        txtstream.WriteLine("<BODY bgcolor=navy Topmargin=0
TEXT=""Black"" LINK=""#993366"" VLINK=""#660066""
ALINK=""#FF99FF"" margin-right=10px>")
        txtstream.WriteLine("<TABLE
style=""Position:Absolute;Top:50;Left:0;Font-family:Tahoma;font-
size:10px"">")
        txtstream.WriteLine("<TR><TH>")
        txtstream.WriteLine("    <v:roundrect id=""A""
style=""width:180;height:30px"" arcsize=""5%"">   ")
        txtstream.WriteLine("    <v:fill color=""Silver""
color2=""white"" Opacity=100%  Opacity2=100% angle=""0""
type=""gradient"" />")
        txtstream.WriteLine("    <v:textbox id=""A1""
style=""font-family:Garmond;Font-size:10px;Color:DarkRed"">" &
ComboBox1.Text & "</v:textbox>")
        txtstream.WriteLine("    <v:shadow id=""A2"" on=""True""
offset=""3pt, 3pt"" opacity=""70%"" color=""navy""/>")
        txtstream.WriteLine("    </v:roundrect>")
        txtstream.WriteLine("</TH></TR>")
        txtstream.WriteLine("</TABLE>")
        txtstream.WriteLine("<table cellspacing=2px
cellpadding=2px rules=all frames=both Class=""myclass1""
style='Position:Absolute;Left:5px;Top:75px;width:100%;height:400p
x;Background-color:white;color:navy;font-size:12px;font-
family:Courier New;Width:100%;height:100%'>")


        Using R As
System.Management.Automation.Runspaces.Runspace =
System.Management.Automation.Runspaces.RunspaceFactory.CreateRuns
pace()
```

```vb
        'Create the pipeline
        Using P As
System.Management.Automation.Runspaces.Pipeline =
R.CreatePipeline()

            'Open the runspace.
            R.Open()

            'Create each command (in this case just one)...

            Dim tstr As String = "$Data = Get-" &
ComboBox1.Text & " | Format-Table -Autosize | Out-String -Width
4096" & vbCrLf
            tstr = tstr & "$Data" & vbCrLf

            Dim Cmd As New
System.Management.Automation.Runspaces.Command(tstr, True)

            '...and add it to the pipeline.
            P.Commands.Add(Cmd)

P.Commands(0).MergeMyResults(PipelineResultTypes.Error,
PipelineResultTypes.Output)
            'Execute the commands and get the response.
            Dim Result As
System.Collections.ObjectModel.Collection(Of _
            System.Management.Automation.PSObject) =
P.Invoke()

            txtstream.WriteLine("<tr><td valign=top><pre
style='Background-color:white;color:navy;font-size:12px;font-
family:Courier New;' align=left nowrap>")

            For Each O As
System.Management.Automation.PSObject In Result
                'Display the result in the console window.
                Try
                    txtstream.Writeline(O.ToString())
                Catch ex As Exception
                    txtstream.Writeline(ex.Message)
                End Try
            Next

        End Using
```

```
            'Close the runspace.
            R.Close()

        End Using



        txtstream.WriteLine("</pre></td></tr>")
        txtstream.WriteLine("</div>")
        txtstream.WriteLine("</body>")
        txtstream.WriteLine("</html>")
        txtstream.WriteLine("")
        txtstream.Close()

        WebBrowser1.Navigate(Application.StartupPath & "\" &
ComboBox1.Text & ".htm")
    End Sub
End Class
```

Below is a list of cmdlets that PowerShell has and you can try then with the program above:

ADAccountAuthorizationGroup
ADAccountResultantPasswordReplicationPolicy
ADAuthenticationPolicy
ADAuthenticationPolicySilo
ADCentralAccessPolicy
ADCentralAccessRule
ADClaimTransformPolicy
ADClaimType
ADComputer
ADComputerServiceAccount
ADDCCloningExcludedApplicationList
ADDefaultDomainPasswordPolicy
ADDomain
ADDomainController
ADDomainControllerPasswordReplicationPolicy

ADDomainControllerPasswordReplicationPolicy...
ADFineGrainedPasswordPolicy
ADFineGrainedPasswordPolicySubject
ADForest
ADGroup
ADGroupMember
ADObject
ADOptionalFeature
ADOrganizationalUnit
ADPrincipalGroupMembership
ADReplicationAttributeMetadata
ADReplicationConnection
ADReplicationFailure
ADReplicationPartnerMetadata
ADReplicationQueueOperation
ADReplicationSite
ADReplicationSiteLink
ADReplicationSiteLinkBridge
ADReplicationSubnet
ADReplicationUpToDatenessVectorTable
ADResourceProperty
ADResourcePropertyList
ADResourcePropertyValueType
ADRootDSE
ADServiceAccount
ADTrust
ADUser
ADUserResultantPasswordPolicy
DhcpServerAuditLog
DhcpServerDatabase
DhcpServerDnsCredential
DhcpServerInDC
DhcpServerSetting
DhcpServerv4Binding
DhcpServerv4Class

DhcpServerv4DnsSetting
DhcpServerv4ExclusionRange
DhcpServerv4Failover
DhcpServerv4Filter
DhcpServerv4FilterList
DhcpServerv4FreeIPAddress
DhcpServerv4Lease
DhcpServerv4MulticastExclusionRange
DhcpServerv4MulticastLease
DhcpServerv4MulticastScope
DhcpServerv4MulticastScopeStatistics
DhcpServerv4OptionDefinition
DhcpServerv4OptionValue
DhcpServerv4Policy
DhcpServerv4PolicyIPRange
DhcpServerv4Reservation
DhcpServerv4Scope
DhcpServerv4ScopeStatistics
DhcpServerv4Statistics
DhcpServerv4Superscope
DhcpServerv4SuperScopeStatistics
DhcpServerv6Binding
DhcpServerv6Class
DhcpServerv6DnsSetting
DhcpServerv6ExclusionRange
DhcpServerv6FreeIPAddress
DhcpServerv6Lease
DhcpServerv6OptionDefinition
DhcpServerv6OptionValue
DhcpServerv6Reservation
DhcpServerv6Scope
DhcpServerv6ScopeStatistics
DhcpServerv6StatelessStatistics
DhcpServerv6StatelessStore
DhcpServerv6Statistics

DhcpServerVersion
DnsClient
DnsClientCache
DnsClientGlobalSetting
DnsClientNrptGlobal
DnsClientNrptPolicy
DnsClientNrptRule
DnsClientServerAddress
DnsServer
DnsServerCache
DnsServerDiagnostics
DnsServerDirectoryPartition
DnsServerDnsSecZoneSetting
DnsServerDsSetting
DnsServerEDns
DnsServerForwarder
DnsServerGlobalNameZone
DnsServerGlobalQueryBlockList
DnsServerRecursion
DnsServerResourceRecord
DnsServerRootHint
DnsServerScavenging
DnsServerSetting
DnsServerSigningKey
DnsServerStatistics
DnsServerTrustAnchor
DnsServerTrustPoint
DnsServerZone
DnsServerZoneAging
DnsServerZoneDelegation
GPO
GPOReport
GPPermission
GPPrefRegistryValue
GPRegistryValue

GPResultantSetOfPolicy
GPStarterGPO
IMAP
IpamAddress
IpamAddressSpace
IpamAddressUtilizationThreshold
IpamBlock
IpamCapability
IpamConfiguration
IpamConfigurationEvent
IpamCustomField
IpamCustomFieldAssociation
IpamDatabase
IpamDhcpConfigurationEvent
IpamDiscoveryDomain
IpamIpAddressAuditEvent
IpamRange
IpamServerInventory
IpamSubnet
Job
JobTrigger
KdsConfiguration
KdsRootKey
LDAP
MsmqCertificate
MsmqOutgoingQueue
MsmqQueue
MsmqQueueACL
MsmqQueueManager
MsmqQueueManagerACL
Net6to4Configuration
NetAdapter
NetAdapterAdvancedProperty
NetAdapterBinding
NetAdapterChecksumOffload

NetAdapterEncapsulatedPacketTaskOffload
NetAdapterHardwareInfo
NetAdapterIPsecOffload
NetAdapterLso
NetAdapterPowerManagement
NetAdapterQos
NetAdapterRdma
NetAdapterRsc
NetAdapterRss
NetAdapterSriov
NetAdapterSriovVf
NetAdapterStatistics
NetAdapterVmq
NetAdapterVMQQueue
NetAdapterVPort
NetCompartment
NetConnectionProfile
NetDnsTransitionConfiguration
NetDnsTransitionMonitoring
NetEventNetworkAdapter
NetEventPacketCaptureProvider
NetEventProvider
NetEventSession
NetEventVmNetworkAdapter
NetEventVmSwitch
NetFirewallAddressFilter
NetFirewallApplicationFilter
NetFirewallInterfaceFilter
NetFirewallInterfaceTypeFilter
NetFirewallPortFilter
NetFirewallProfile
NetFirewallRule
NetFirewallSecurityFilter
NetFirewallServiceFilter
NetFirewallSetting

NetIPAddress
NetIPConfiguration
NetIPHttpsConfiguration
NetIPHttpsState
NetIPInterface
NetIPsecDospSetting
NetIPsecMainModeCryptoSet
NetIPsecMainModeRule
NetIPsecMainModeSA
NetIPsecPhase1AuthSet
NetIPsecPhase2AuthSet
NetIPsecQuickModeCryptoSet
NetIPsecQuickModeSA
NetIPsecRule
NetIPv4Protocol
NetIPv6Protocol
NetIsatapConfiguration
NetLbfoTeam
NetLbfoTeamMember
NetLbfoTeamNic
NetNeighbor
NetOffloadGlobalSetting
NetPrefixPolicy
NetQosPolicy
NetRoute
NetSwitchTeam
NetSwitchTeamMember
NetTCPConnection
NetTCPSetting
NetTeredoConfiguration
NetTeredoState
NetTransportFilter
NetUDPEndpoint
NetUDPSetting
Packet

RAS
RSS
ScheduledJob
ScheduledJobOption
VpnAuthProtocol
VpnConnection
VpnConnectionTrigger
VpnS2SInterface
VpnS2SInterfaceStatistics
VpnServerConfiguration
WebAppDomain
WebApplication
WebAppPoolState
WebBinding
WebCentralCertProvider
WebConfigFile
WebConfiguration
WebConfigurationBackup
WebConfigurationLocation
WebConfigurationLock
WebConfigurationProperty
WebDAV
WebFilePath
WebGlobalModule
WebHandler
WebItemState
WebManagedModule
WebRequest
Website
WebsiteState
WebURL
WebVirtualDirectory
WheaMemoryPolicy
Whois
WIMBootEntry

WinAcceptLanguageFromLanguageListOptOut
WinCultureFromLanguageListOptOut
WinDefaultInputMethodOverride
WindowsDriver
WindowsEdition
WindowsErrorReporting
WindowsImage
WindowsImageContent
WindowsOptionalFeature
WindowsPackage
WindowsSearchSetting
WinEvent
WinHomeLocation
WinLanguageBarOption
WinSystemLocale
WinUILanguageOverride
WinUserLanguageList
WsusClassification
WsusComputer
WsusProduct
WsusServer
WsusUpdate

Network Drive Functions

Map Network Drive

```
Private Sub MapNetworkDrive()

    Dim x As Integer = 0
    x = WNetConnectionDialog(Me.Handle.ToInt32, 1)

End Sub
```

Disconnect Network Drive

```
Private Sub DisconnectNetworkDrive()

    Dim x As Integer = 0
    x = WNetDisconnectDialog(Me.Handle.ToInt32, 1)

End Sub
```

ShellExecute Functions

Open Access

```
    Dim   x   As   Integer   =   ShellExecute(Me.Handle.ToInt32,   "Open",
"MSAccess.exe", "", "", 1)
```

Open Calculator

```
    Dim x As Integer = ShellExecute(Me.Handle.ToInt32, "Open", "Calc.exe",
"", "", 1)
```

Open DxDiag

```
    Dim x As Integer = ShellExecute(Me.Handle.ToInt32, "Open", "dxdiag.exe",
"", "", 1)
```

Open Excel

```
    Dim x As Integer = ShellExecute(Me.Handle.ToInt32, "Open", "Excel.exe",
"", "", 1)
```

Open Magnifier

```
Dim x As Integer = ShellExecute(Me.Handle.ToInt32, "Open",
"magnify.exe", "", "", 1)
```

Open Notepad

```
Dim x As Integer = ShellExecute(Me.Handle.ToInt32, "Open",
"Notepad.exe", "", "", 1)
```

Open Outlook

```
Dim x As Integer = ShellExecute(Me.Handle.ToInt32, "Open",
"Outlook.exe", "", "", 1)
```

Open DateTime

```
Dim x As Integer = Shell("rundll32.exe shell32.dll,Control_RunDLL
timedate.cpl,,0")
```

Open Word

```
Dim x As Integer = ShellExecute(Me.Handle.ToInt32, "Open",
"Winword.exe", "", "", 1)
```

Open WordPad

```
Dim x As Integer = ShellExecute(Me.Handle.ToInt32, "Open",
"Wordpad.exe", "", "", 1)
```

Open DCOMConfig

```
Dim x As Integer = ShellExecute(Me.Handle.ToInt32, "Open",
"dcomcnfg.exe", "", "", 1)
```

Open Command Prompt

```
Dim x As Integer = ShellExecute(Me.Handle.ToInt32, "Open", "cmd.exe", "",
"", 1)
```

Open PowerShell

```
Dim x As Integer = ShellExecute(Me.Handle.ToInt32, "Open",
"Powershell.exe", "", "", 1)
```

Open Regedit

```
Dim x As Integer = ShellExecute(Me.Handle.ToInt32, "Open", "Regedit.exe",
"", "", 1)
```

Mail Functions

GMAIL

This is the code for Gmail. I've tested it with my credentials and it works. Remember, the focus of this book is on making COM work. And, yes, this is a converted VBScript:

```vbscript
Dim EmailSubject
Dim EmailBody

EmailSubject = ""              'create a subject text. Like this is a test.
EmailBody = ""                 'Add some body text

Const EmailFrom = ""           'Your current gmail e-mail address
Const EmailFromName = ""       'Your screen name can work
Const EmailTo = ""             'who you want to sned mail to
Const SMTPServer = "smtp.gmail.com"
Const SMTPLogon = ""           'Your Gmail sigon name
Const SMTPPassword = "gMailPaSsWoRd"    'Your Gmail sigon password
Const SMTPSSL = True
Const SMTPPort = 465

Const cdoSendUsingPickup = 1     'Send message using local SMTP service pickup directory.
Const cdoSendUsingPort = 2       'Send the message using SMTP over TCP/IP networking.
Const cdoAnonymous = 0           'No authentication
Const cdoBasic = 1               'BASIC clear text authentication
Const cdoNTLM = 2                'NTLM, Microsoft proprietary authentication

                'First, create the message

Set oMsg = CreateObject("CDO.Message")
oMsg.Subject = EmailSubject
oMsg.From = """" & EmailFromName & """" <" & EmailFrom & ">"
oMsg.To = EmailTo
oMsg.TextBody = EmailBody

                'Second, configure the server

oMsg.Configuration.Fields.Item("http://schemas.microsoft.com/cdo/configuration/sendusing") = 2
oMsg.Configuration.Fields.Item("http://schemas.microsoft.com/cdo/configuration/smtpserver") = SMTPServer
oMsg.Configuration.Fields.Item("http://schemas.microsoft.com/cdo/configuration/smtpauthenticate") = cdoBasic
oMsg.Configuration.Fields.Item("http://schemas.microsoft.com/cdo/configuration/sendusername") = SMTPLogon
oMsg.Configuration.Fields.Item("http://schemas.microsoft.com/cdo/configuration/sendpassword") = SMTPPassword
oMsg.Configuration.Fields.Item("http://schemas.microsoft.com/cdo/configuration/smtpserverport") = SMTPPort
oMsg.Configuration.Fields.Item("http://schemas.microsoft.com/cdo/configuration/smtpusessl") = SMTPSSL
oMsg.Configuration.Fields.Item("http://schemas.microsoft.com/cdo/configuration/smtpconnectiontimeout") = 60
Call oMsg.Configuration.Fields.Update

On Error Resume Next
Call oMsg.Send

iret = MsgBox("Mail was successfully sent !", 64, "Information")
If Err.Number <> 0 Then
  MsgBox ("There was an error sending mail. The error Message is: " & Err.Description)
  Err.Clear
End If
```

I sent this one to myself:

Now, let's do Outlook Mail

Outlook Mail

Okay, here's the Outlook code:

```
Set oOutlook = CreateObject("Outlook.Application")
Set Mapi = oOutlook.GetNamespace("MAPI")
Mapi.Logon("Default OutlookProfile",, False, False)

Set oMail = oOutlook.CreateItem(0)
oMail.To = ""          'Who you want to send mail to
oMail.Subject = ""     'Your subject goes here
oMail.Body = ""         'The body of the message you
want to send

oMail.Send()           'Tell mail you want to send it
oOutlook.Quit()        'Tell Outlook to close
```

I used my Hotmail account to send an e-mail to my Gmail Account:

A few words about sending mail with Outlook. Expect a nag screen to show up when you send mail through Outlook.

See that was a few words.

Stylesheets
Decorating your web pages

BELOW ARE SOME STYLESHEETS I COOKED UP THAT I LIKE AND THINK YOU MIGHT TOO. Don't worry I won't be offended if you take and modify to your hearts delight. Please do!

NONE

```
txtstream.WriteLine("<style type='text/css'>")
txtstream.WriteLine("th")
txtstream.WriteLine("{")
txtstream.WriteLine("    COLOR: white;")
txtstream.WriteLine("}")
txtstream.WriteLine("td")
txtstream.WriteLine("{")
txtstream.WriteLine("    COLOR: white;")
txtstream.WriteLine("}")
txtstream.WriteLine("</style>")
```

BLACK AND WHITE TEXT

```
txtstream.WriteLine("<style type='text/css'>")
txtstream.WriteLine("th")
txtstream.WriteLine("{")
txtstream.WriteLine("   COLOR: white;")
txtstream.WriteLine("   BACKGROUND-COLOR: black;")
txtstream.WriteLine("   FONT-FAMILY:font-family: Cambria, serif;")
txtstream.WriteLine("   FONT-SIZE: 12px;")
txtstream.WriteLine("   text-align: left;")
txtstream.WriteLine("   white-Space: nowrap;")
txtstream.WriteLine("}")
txtstream.WriteLine("td")
txtstream.WriteLine("{")
txtstream.WriteLine("   COLOR: white;")
txtstream.WriteLine("   BACKGROUND-COLOR: black;")
txtstream.WriteLine("   FONT-FAMILY: font-family: Cambria, serif;")
txtstream.WriteLine("   FONT-SIZE: 12px;")
txtstream.WriteLine("   text-align: left;")
txtstream.WriteLine("   white-Space: nowrap;")
txtstream.WriteLine("}")
txtstream.WriteLine("div")
txtstream.WriteLine("{")
txtstream.WriteLine("   COLOR: white;")
txtstream.WriteLine("   BACKGROUND-COLOR: black;")
txtstream.WriteLine("   FONT-FAMILY: font-family: Cambria, serif;")
txtstream.WriteLine("   FONT-SIZE: 10px;")
txtstream.WriteLine("   text-align: left;")
txtstream.WriteLine("   white-Space: nowrap;")
txtstream.WriteLine("}")
txtstream.WriteLine("span")
txtstream.WriteLine("{")
```

```
txtstream.WriteLine("    COLOR: white;")
txtstream.WriteLine("    BACKGROUND-COLOR: black;")
txtstream.WriteLine("    FONT-FAMILY: font-family: Cambria, serif;")
txtstream.WriteLine("    FONT-SIZE: 10px;")
txtstream.WriteLine("    text-align: left;")
txtstream.WriteLine("    white-Space: nowrap;")
txtstream.WriteLine("    display:inline-block;")
txtstream.WriteLine("    width: 100%;")
txtstream.WriteLine("}")
txtstream.WriteLine("textarea")
txtstream.WriteLine("{")
txtstream.WriteLine("    COLOR: white;")
txtstream.WriteLine("    BACKGROUND-COLOR: black;")
txtstream.WriteLine("    FONT-FAMILY: font-family: Cambria, serif;")
txtstream.WriteLine("    FONT-SIZE: 10px;")
txtstream.WriteLine("    text-align: left;")
txtstream.WriteLine("    white-Space: nowrap;")
txtstream.WriteLine("    width: 100%;")
txtstream.WriteLine("}")
txtstream.WriteLine("select")
txtstream.WriteLine("{")
txtstream.WriteLine("    COLOR: white;")
txtstream.WriteLine("    BACKGROUND-COLOR: black;")
txtstream.WriteLine("    FONT-FAMILY: font-family: Cambria, serif;")
txtstream.WriteLine("    FONT-SIZE: 10px;")
txtstream.WriteLine("    text-align: left;")
txtstream.WriteLine("    white-Space: nowrap;")
txtstream.WriteLine("    width: 100%;")
txtstream.WriteLine("}")
txtstream.WriteLine("input")
txtstream.WriteLine("{")
txtstream.WriteLine("    COLOR: white;")
txtstream.WriteLine("    BACKGROUND-COLOR: black;")
```

```
txtstream.WriteLine("    FONT-FAMILY: font-family: Cambria, serif;")
txtstream.WriteLine("    FONT-SIZE: 12px;")
txtstream.WriteLine("    text-align: left;")
txtstream.WriteLine("    display:table-cell;")
txtstream.WriteLine("    white-Space: nowrap;")
txtstream.WriteLine("}")
txtstream.WriteLine("h1 {")
txtstream.WriteLine("color: antiquewhite;")
txtstream.WriteLine("text-shadow: 1px 1px 1px black;")
txtstream.WriteLine("padding: 3px;")
txtstream.WriteLine("text-align: center;")
txtstream.WriteLine("box-shadow: inset 2px 2px 5px rgba(0,0,0,0.5), inset -
2px -2px 5px rgba(255,255,255,0.5);")
txtstream.WriteLine("}")
txtstream.WriteLine("</style>")
```

COLORED TEXT

```
txtstream.WriteLine("<style type='text/css'>")
txtstream.WriteLine("th")
txtstream.WriteLine("{")
txtstream.WriteLine("    COLOR: darkred;")
txtstream.WriteLine("    BACKGROUND-COLOR: #eeeeee;")
txtstream.WriteLine("    FONT-FAMILY:font-family: Cambria, serif;")
txtstream.WriteLine("    FONT-SIZE: 12px;")
txtstream.WriteLine("    text-align: left;")
txtstream.WriteLine("    white-Space: nowrap;")
txtstream.WriteLine("}")
txtstream.WriteLine("td")
txtstream.WriteLine("{")
txtstream.WriteLine("    COLOR: navy;")
txtstream.WriteLine("    BACKGROUND-COLOR: #eeeeee;")
txtstream.WriteLine("    FONT-FAMILY: font-family: Cambria, serif;")
```

```
txtstream.WriteLine("    FONT-SIZE: 12px;")
txtstream.WriteLine("    text-align: left;")
txtstream.WriteLine("    white-Space: nowrap;")
txtstream.WriteLine("}")
txtstream.WriteLine("div")
txtstream.WriteLine("{")
txtstream.WriteLine("    COLOR: white;")
txtstream.WriteLine("    BACKGROUND-COLOR: navy;")
txtstream.WriteLine("    FONT-FAMILY: font-family: Cambria, serif;")
txtstream.WriteLine("    FONT-SIZE: 10px;")
txtstream.WriteLine("    text-align: left;")
txtstream.WriteLine("    white-Space: nowrap;")
txtstream.WriteLine("}")
txtstream.WriteLine("span")
txtstream.WriteLine("{")
txtstream.WriteLine("    COLOR: white;")
txtstream.WriteLine("    BACKGROUND-COLOR: navy;")
txtstream.WriteLine("    FONT-FAMILY: font-family: Cambria, serif;")
txtstream.WriteLine("    FONT-SIZE: 10px;")
txtstream.WriteLine("    text-align: left;")
txtstream.WriteLine("    white-Space: nowrap;")
txtstream.WriteLine("    display:inline-block;")
txtstream.WriteLine("    width: 100%;")
txtstream.WriteLine("}")
txtstream.WriteLine("textarea")
txtstream.WriteLine("{")
txtstream.WriteLine("    COLOR: white;")
txtstream.WriteLine("    BACKGROUND-COLOR: navy;")
txtstream.WriteLine("    FONT-FAMILY: font-family: Cambria, serif;")
txtstream.WriteLine("    FONT-SIZE: 10px;")
txtstream.WriteLine("    text-align: left;")
txtstream.WriteLine("    white-Space: nowrap;")
txtstream.WriteLine("    width: 100%;")
```

```
txtstream.WriteLine("}")
txtstream.WriteLine("select")
txtstream.WriteLine("{")
txtstream.WriteLine("   COLOR: white;")
txtstream.WriteLine("   BACKGROUND-COLOR: navy;")
txtstream.WriteLine("   FONT-FAMILY: font-family: Cambria, serif;")
txtstream.WriteLine("   FONT-SIZE: 10px;")
txtstream.WriteLine("   text-align: left;")
txtstream.WriteLine("   white-Space: nowrap;")
txtstream.WriteLine("   width: 100%;")
txtstream.WriteLine("}")
txtstream.WriteLine("input")
txtstream.WriteLine("{")
txtstream.WriteLine("   COLOR: white;")
txtstream.WriteLine("   BACKGROUND-COLOR: navy;")
txtstream.WriteLine("   FONT-FAMILY: font-family: Cambria, serif;")
txtstream.WriteLine("   FONT-SIZE: 12px;")
txtstream.WriteLine("   text-align: left;")
txtstream.WriteLine("   display:table-cell;")
txtstream.WriteLine("   white-Space: nowrap;")
txtstream.WriteLine("}")
txtstream.WriteLine("h1 {")
txtstream.WriteLine("color: antiquewhite;")
txtstream.WriteLine("text-shadow: 1px 1px 1px black;")
txtstream.WriteLine("padding: 3px;")
txtstream.WriteLine("text-align: center;")
txtstream.WriteLine("box-shadow: inset 2px 2px 5px rgba(0,0,0,0.5), inset -
2px -2px 5px rgba(255,255,255,0.5);")
txtstream.WriteLine("}")
txtstream.WriteLine("</style>")
```

```
txtstream.WriteLine("<style>")
txtstream.WriteLine("th")
txtstream.WriteLine("{")
txtstream.WriteLine("    COLOR: white;")
txtstream.WriteLine("    BACKGROUND-COLOR: navy;")
txtstream.WriteLine("    FONT-FAMILY:font-family: Cambria, serif;")
txtstream.WriteLine("    FONT-SIZE: 12px;")
txtstream.WriteLine("    text-align: left;")
txtstream.WriteLine("    white-Space: nowrap;")
txtstream.WriteLine("}")
txtstream.WriteLine("td")
txtstream.WriteLine("{")
txtstream.WriteLine("    COLOR: navy;")
txtstream.WriteLine("    FONT-FAMILY: font-family: Cambria, serif;")
txtstream.WriteLine("    FONT-SIZE: 12px;")
txtstream.WriteLine("    text-align: left;")
txtstream.WriteLine("    white-Space: nowrap;")
txtstream.WriteLine("}")
txtstream.WriteLine("div")
txtstream.WriteLine("{")
txtstream.WriteLine("    COLOR: navy;")
txtstream.WriteLine("    FONT-FAMILY: font-family: Cambria, serif;")
txtstream.WriteLine("    FONT-SIZE: 12px;")
txtstream.WriteLine("    text-align: left;")
txtstream.WriteLine("    white-Space: nowrap;")
txtstream.WriteLine("}")
txtstream.WriteLine("span")
txtstream.WriteLine("{")
txtstream.WriteLine("    COLOR: navy;")
txtstream.WriteLine("    FONT-FAMILY: font-family: Cambria, serif;")
```

```
txtstream.WriteLine("    FONT-SIZE: 12px;")
txtstream.WriteLine("    text-align: left;")
txtstream.WriteLine("    white-Space: nowrap;")
txtstream.WriteLine("    width: 100%;")
txtstream.WriteLine("}")
txtstream.WriteLine("textarea")
txtstream.WriteLine("{")
txtstream.WriteLine("    COLOR: navy;")
txtstream.WriteLine("    FONT-FAMILY: font-family: Cambria, serif;")
txtstream.WriteLine("    FONT-SIZE: 12px;")
txtstream.WriteLine("    text-align: left;")
txtstream.WriteLine("    white-Space: nowrap;")
txtstream.WriteLine("    display:inline-block;")
txtstream.WriteLine("    width: 100%;")
txtstream.WriteLine("}")
txtstream.WriteLine("select")
txtstream.WriteLine("{")
txtstream.WriteLine("    COLOR: navy;")
txtstream.WriteLine("    FONT-FAMILY: font-family: Cambria, serif;")
txtstream.WriteLine("    FONT-SIZE: 10px;")
txtstream.WriteLine("    text-align: left;")
txtstream.WriteLine("    white-Space: nowrap;")
txtstream.WriteLine("    display:inline-block;")
txtstream.WriteLine("    width: 100%;")
txtstream.WriteLine("}")
txtstream.WriteLine("input")
txtstream.WriteLine("{")
txtstream.WriteLine("    COLOR: navy;")
txtstream.WriteLine("    FONT-FAMILY: font-family: Cambria, serif;")
txtstream.WriteLine("    FONT-SIZE: 12px;")
txtstream.WriteLine("    text-align: left;")
txtstream.WriteLine("    display:table-cell;")
txtstream.WriteLine("    white-Space: nowrap;")
```

```
txtstream.WriteLine("}")
txtstream.WriteLine("h1 {")
txtstream.WriteLine("color: antiquewhite;")
txtstream.WriteLine("text-shadow: 1px 1px 1px black;")
txtstream.WriteLine("padding: 3px;")
txtstream.WriteLine("text-align: center;")
txtstream.WriteLine("box-shadow: inset 2px 2px 5px rgba(0,0,0,0.5), inset -
2px -2px 5px rgba(255,255,255,0.5);")
txtstream.WriteLine("}")
txtstream.WriteLine("tr:nth-child(even){background-color:#f2f2f2;}")
txtstream.WriteLine("tr:nth-child(odd){background-color:#cccccc;
color:#f2f2f2;}")
txtstream.WriteLine("</style>")
```

GHOST DECORATED

```
txtstream.WriteLine("<style type='text/css'>")
txtstream.WriteLine("th")
txtstream.WriteLine("{")
txtstream.WriteLine("   COLOR: black;")
txtstream.WriteLine("   BACKGROUND-COLOR: white;")
txtstream.WriteLine("   FONT-FAMILY:font-family: Cambria, serif;")
txtstream.WriteLine("   FONT-SIZE: 12px;")
txtstream.WriteLine("   text-align: left;")
txtstream.WriteLine("   white-Space: nowrap;")
txtstream.WriteLine("}")
txtstream.WriteLine("td")
txtstream.WriteLine("{")
txtstream.WriteLine("   COLOR: black;")
txtstream.WriteLine("   BACKGROUND-COLOR: white;")
txtstream.WriteLine("   FONT-FAMILY: font-family: Cambria, serif;")
txtstream.WriteLine("   FONT-SIZE: 12px;")
txtstream.WriteLine("   text-align: left;")
```

```
txtstream.WriteLine("    white-Space: nowrap;")
txtstream.WriteLine("}")
txtstream.WriteLine("div")
txtstream.WriteLine("{")
txtstream.WriteLine("    COLOR: black;")
txtstream.WriteLine("    BACKGROUND-COLOR: white;")
txtstream.WriteLine("    FONT-FAMILY: font-family: Cambria, serif;")
txtstream.WriteLine("    FONT-SIZE: 10px;")
txtstream.WriteLine("    text-align: left;")
txtstream.WriteLine("    white-Space: nowrap;")
txtstream.WriteLine("}")
txtstream.WriteLine("span")
txtstream.WriteLine("{")
txtstream.WriteLine("    COLOR: black;")
txtstream.WriteLine("    BACKGROUND-COLOR: white;")
txtstream.WriteLine("    FONT-FAMILY: font-family: Cambria, serif;")
txtstream.WriteLine("    FONT-SIZE: 10px;")
txtstream.WriteLine("    text-align: left;")
txtstream.WriteLine("    white-Space: nowrap;")
txtstream.WriteLine("    display:inline-block;")
txtstream.WriteLine("    width: 100%;")
txtstream.WriteLine("}")
txtstream.WriteLine("textarea")
txtstream.WriteLine("{")
txtstream.WriteLine("    COLOR: black;")
txtstream.WriteLine("    BACKGROUND-COLOR: white;")
txtstream.WriteLine("    FONT-FAMILY: font-family: Cambria, serif;")
txtstream.WriteLine("    FONT-SIZE: 10px;")
txtstream.WriteLine("    text-align: left;")
txtstream.WriteLine("    white-Space: nowrap;")
txtstream.WriteLine("    width: 100%;")
txtstream.WriteLine("}")
txtstream.WriteLine("select")
```

```
txtstream.WriteLine("{")
txtstream.WriteLine("    COLOR: black;")
txtstream.WriteLine("    BACKGROUND-COLOR: white;")
txtstream.WriteLine("    FONT-FAMILY: font-family: Cambria, serif;")
txtstream.WriteLine("    FONT-SIZE: 10px;")
txtstream.WriteLine("    text-align: left;")
txtstream.WriteLine("    white-Space: nowrap;")
txtstream.WriteLine("    width: 100%;")
txtstream.WriteLine("}")
txtstream.WriteLine("input")
txtstream.WriteLine("{")
txtstream.WriteLine("    COLOR: black;")
txtstream.WriteLine("    BACKGROUND-COLOR: white;")
txtstream.WriteLine("    FONT-FAMILY: font-family: Cambria, serif;")
txtstream.WriteLine("    FONT-SIZE: 12px;")
txtstream.WriteLine("    text-align: left;")
txtstream.WriteLine("    display:table-cell;")
txtstream.WriteLine("    white-Space: nowrap;")
txtstream.WriteLine("}")
txtstream.WriteLine("h1 {")
txtstream.WriteLine("color: antiquewhite;")
txtstream.WriteLine("text-shadow: 1px 1px 1px black;")
txtstream.WriteLine("padding: 3px;")
txtstream.WriteLine("text-align: center;")
txtstream.WriteLine("box-shadow: inset 2px 2px 5px rgba(0,0,0,0.5), inset -
2px -2px 5px rgba(255,255,255,0.5);")
txtstream.WriteLine("}")
txtstream.WriteLine("</style>")
```

3D

```
txtstream.WriteLine("<style type='text/css'>")
```

```
txtstream.WriteLine("body")
txtstream.WriteLine("{")
txtstream.WriteLine("   PADDING-RIGHT: 0px;")
txtstream.WriteLine("   PADDING-LEFT: 0px;")
txtstream.WriteLine("   PADDING-BOTTOM: 0px;")
txtstream.WriteLine("   MARGIN: 0px;")
txtstream.WriteLine("   COLOR: #333;")
txtstream.WriteLine("   PADDING-TOP: 0px;")
txtstream.WriteLine("   FONT-FAMILY: verdana, arial, helvetica, sans-serif;")
txtstream.WriteLine("}")
txtstream.WriteLine("table")
txtstream.WriteLine("{")
txtstream.WriteLine("   BORDER-RIGHT: #999999 3px solid;")
txtstream.WriteLine("   PADDING-RIGHT: 6px;")
txtstream.WriteLine("   PADDING-LEFT: 6px;")
txtstream.WriteLine("   FONT-WEIGHT: Bold;")
txtstream.WriteLine("   FONT-SIZE: 14px;")
txtstream.WriteLine("   PADDING-BOTTOM: 6px;")
txtstream.WriteLine("   COLOR: Peru;")
txtstream.WriteLine("   LINE-HEIGHT: 14px;")
txtstream.WriteLine("   PADDING-TOP: 6px;")
txtstream.WriteLine("   BORDER-BOTTOM: #999 1px solid;")
txtstream.WriteLine("   BACKGROUND-COLOR: #eeeeee;")
txtstream.WriteLine("   FONT-FAMILY: verdana, arial, helvetica, sans-serif;")
txtstream.WriteLine("   FONT-SIZE: 12px;")
txtstream.WriteLine("}")
txtstream.WriteLine("th")
txtstream.WriteLine("{")
txtstream.WriteLine("   BORDER-RIGHT: #999999 3px solid;")
txtstream.WriteLine("   PADDING-RIGHT: 6px;")
txtstream.WriteLine("   PADDING-LEFT: 6px;")
txtstream.WriteLine("   FONT-WEIGHT: Bold;")
txtstream.WriteLine("   FONT-SIZE: 14px;")
```

```
txtstream.WriteLine("    PADDING-BOTTOM: 6px;")
txtstream.WriteLine("    COLOR: darkred;")
txtstream.WriteLine("    LINE-HEIGHT: 14px;")
txtstream.WriteLine("    PADDING-TOP: 6px;")
txtstream.WriteLine("    BORDER-BOTTOM: #999 1px solid;")
txtstream.WriteLine("    BACKGROUND-COLOR: #eeeeee;")
txtstream.WriteLine("    FONT-FAMILY:font-family: Cambria, serif;")
txtstream.WriteLine("    FONT-SIZE: 12px;")
txtstream.WriteLine("    text-align: left;")
txtstream.WriteLine("    white-Space: nowrap;")
txtstream.WriteLine("}")
txtstream.WriteLine(".th")
txtstream.WriteLine("{")
txtstream.WriteLine("    BORDER-RIGHT: #999999 2px solid;")
txtstream.WriteLine("    PADDING-RIGHT: 6px;")
txtstream.WriteLine("    PADDING-LEFT: 6px;")
txtstream.WriteLine("    FONT-WEIGHT: Bold;")
txtstream.WriteLine("    PADDING-BOTTOM: 6px;")
txtstream.WriteLine("    COLOR: black;")
txtstream.WriteLine("    PADDING-TOP: 6px;")
txtstream.WriteLine("    BORDER-BOTTOM: #999 2px solid;")
txtstream.WriteLine("    BACKGROUND-COLOR: #eeeeee;")
txtstream.WriteLine("    FONT-FAMILY: font-family: Cambria, serif;")
txtstream.WriteLine("    FONT-SIZE: 10px;")
txtstream.WriteLine("    text-align: right;")
txtstream.WriteLine("    white-Space: nowrap;")
txtstream.WriteLine("}")
txtstream.WriteLine("td")
txtstream.WriteLine("{")
txtstream.WriteLine("    BORDER-RIGHT: #999999 3px solid;")
txtstream.WriteLine("    PADDING-RIGHT: 6px;")
txtstream.WriteLine("    PADDING-LEFT: 6px;")
txtstream.WriteLine("    FONT-WEIGHT: Normal;")
```

```
txtstream.WriteLine("    PADDING-BOTTOM: 6px;")
txtstream.WriteLine("    COLOR: navy;")
txtstream.WriteLine("    LINE-HEIGHT: 14px;")
txtstream.WriteLine("    PADDING-TOP: 6px;")
txtstream.WriteLine("    BORDER-BOTTOM: #999 1px solid;")
txtstream.WriteLine("    BACKGROUND-COLOR: #eeeeee;")
txtstream.WriteLine("    FONT-FAMILY: font-family: Cambria, serif;")
txtstream.WriteLine("    FONT-SIZE: 12px;")
txtstream.WriteLine("    text-align: left;")
txtstream.WriteLine("    white-Space: nowrap;")
txtstream.WriteLine("}")
txtstream.WriteLine("div")
txtstream.WriteLine("{")
txtstream.WriteLine("    BORDER-RIGHT: #999999 3px solid;")
txtstream.WriteLine("    PADDING-RIGHT: 6px;")
txtstream.WriteLine("    PADDING-LEFT: 6px;")
txtstream.WriteLine("    FONT-WEIGHT: Normal;")
txtstream.WriteLine("    PADDING-BOTTOM: 6px;")
txtstream.WriteLine("    COLOR: white;")
txtstream.WriteLine("    PADDING-TOP: 6px;")
txtstream.WriteLine("    BORDER-BOTTOM: #999 1px solid;")
txtstream.WriteLine("    BACKGROUND-COLOR: navy;")
txtstream.WriteLine("    FONT-FAMILY: font-family: Cambria, serif;")
txtstream.WriteLine("    FONT-SIZE: 10px;")
txtstream.WriteLine("    text-align: left;")
txtstream.WriteLine("    white-Space: nowrap;")
txtstream.WriteLine("}")
txtstream.WriteLine("span")
txtstream.WriteLine("{")
txtstream.WriteLine("    BORDER-RIGHT: #999999 3px solid;")
txtstream.WriteLine("    PADDING-RIGHT: 3px;")
txtstream.WriteLine("    PADDING-LEFT: 3px;")
txtstream.WriteLine("    FONT-WEIGHT: Normal;")
```

```
txtstream.WriteLine("    PADDING-BOTTOM: 3px;")
txtstream.WriteLine("    COLOR: white;")
txtstream.WriteLine("    PADDING-TOP: 3px;")
txtstream.WriteLine("    BORDER-BOTTOM: #999 1px solid;")
txtstream.WriteLine("    BACKGROUND-COLOR: navy;")
txtstream.WriteLine("    FONT-FAMILY: font-family: Cambria, serif;")
txtstream.WriteLine("    FONT-SIZE: 10px;")
txtstream.WriteLine("    text-align: left;")
txtstream.WriteLine("    white-Space: nowrap;")
txtstream.WriteLine("    display:inline-block;")
txtstream.WriteLine("    width: 100%;")
txtstream.WriteLine("}")
txtstream.WriteLine("textarea")
txtstream.WriteLine("{")
txtstream.WriteLine("    BORDER-RIGHT: #999999 3px solid;")
txtstream.WriteLine("    PADDING-RIGHT: 3px;")
txtstream.WriteLine("    PADDING-LEFT: 3px;")
txtstream.WriteLine("    FONT-WEIGHT: Normal;")
txtstream.WriteLine("    PADDING-BOTTOM: 3px;")
txtstream.WriteLine("    COLOR: white;")
txtstream.WriteLine("    PADDING-TOP: 3px;")
txtstream.WriteLine("    BORDER-BOTTOM: #999 1px solid;")
txtstream.WriteLine("    BACKGROUND-COLOR: navy;")
txtstream.WriteLine("    FONT-FAMILY: font-family: Cambria, serif;")
txtstream.WriteLine("    FONT-SIZE: 10px;")
txtstream.WriteLine("    text-align: left;")
txtstream.WriteLine("    white-Space: nowrap;")
txtstream.WriteLine("    width: 100%;")
txtstream.WriteLine("}")
txtstream.WriteLine("select")
txtstream.WriteLine("{")
txtstream.WriteLine("    BORDER-RIGHT: #999999 3px solid;")
txtstream.WriteLine("    PADDING-RIGHT: 6px;")
```

```
txtstream.WriteLine("    PADDING-LEFT: 6px;")
txtstream.WriteLine("    FONT-WEIGHT: Normal;")
txtstream.WriteLine("    PADDING-BOTTOM: 6px;")
txtstream.WriteLine("    COLOR: white;")
txtstream.WriteLine("    PADDING-TOP: 6px;")
txtstream.WriteLine("    BORDER-BOTTOM: #999 1px solid;")
txtstream.WriteLine("    BACKGROUND-COLOR: navy;")
txtstream.WriteLine("    FONT-FAMILY: font-family: Cambria, serif;")
txtstream.WriteLine("    FONT-SIZE: 10px;")
txtstream.WriteLine("    text-align: left;")
txtstream.WriteLine("    white-Space: nowrap;")
txtstream.WriteLine("    width: 100%;")
txtstream.WriteLine("}")
txtstream.WriteLine("input")
txtstream.WriteLine("{")
txtstream.WriteLine("    BORDER-RIGHT: #999999 3px solid;")
txtstream.WriteLine("    PADDING-RIGHT: 3px;")
txtstream.WriteLine("    PADDING-LEFT: 3px;")
txtstream.WriteLine("    FONT-WEIGHT: Bold;")
txtstream.WriteLine("    PADDING-BOTTOM: 3px;")
txtstream.WriteLine("    COLOR: white;")
txtstream.WriteLine("    PADDING-TOP: 3px;")
txtstream.WriteLine("    BORDER-BOTTOM: #999 1px solid;")
txtstream.WriteLine("    BACKGROUND-COLOR: navy;")
txtstream.WriteLine("    FONT-FAMILY: font-family: Cambria, serif;")
txtstream.WriteLine("    FONT-SIZE: 12px;")
txtstream.WriteLine("    text-align: left;")
txtstream.WriteLine("    display:table-cell;")
txtstream.WriteLine("    white-Space: nowrap;")
txtstream.WriteLine("    width: 100%;")
txtstream.WriteLine("}")
txtstream.WriteLine("h1 {")
txtstream.WriteLine("color: antiquewhite;")
```

```
txtstream.WriteLine("text-shadow: 1px 1px 1px black;")
txtstream.WriteLine("padding: 3px;")
txtstream.WriteLine("text-align: center;")
txtstream.WriteLine("box-shadow: inset 2px 2px 5px rgba(0,0,0,0.5), inset -
2px -2px 5px rgba(255,255,255,0.5);")
txtstream.WriteLine("}")
txtstream.WriteLine("</style>")
```

SHADOW BOX

```
txtstream.WriteLine("<style type='text/css'>")
txtstream.WriteLine("body")
txtstream.WriteLine("{")
txtstream.WriteLine("   PADDING-RIGHT: 0px;")
txtstream.WriteLine("   PADDING-LEFT: 0px;")
txtstream.WriteLine("   PADDING-BOTTOM: 0px;")
txtstream.WriteLine("   MARGIN: 0px;")
txtstream.WriteLine("   COLOR: #333;")
txtstream.WriteLine("   PADDING-TOP: 0px;")
txtstream.WriteLine("   FONT-FAMILY: verdana, arial, helvetica, sans-serif;")
txtstream.WriteLine("}")
txtstream.WriteLine("table")
txtstream.WriteLine("{")
txtstream.WriteLine("   BORDER-RIGHT: #999999 1px solid;")
txtstream.WriteLine("   PADDING-RIGHT: 1px;")
txtstream.WriteLine("   PADDING-LEFT: 1px;")
txtstream.WriteLine("   PADDING-BOTTOM: 1px;")
txtstream.WriteLine("   LINE-HEIGHT: 8px;")
txtstream.WriteLine("   PADDING-TOP: 1px;")
txtstream.WriteLine("   BORDER-BOTTOM: #999 1px solid;")
txtstream.WriteLine("   BACKGROUND-COLOR: #eeeeee;")
```

```
        txtstream.WriteLine("
filter:progid:DXImageTransform.Microsoft.Shadow(color='silver',          Direction=135,
Strength=16")
    txtstream.WriteLine("}")
    txtstream.WriteLine("th")
    txtstream.WriteLine("{")
    txtstream.WriteLine("    BORDER-RIGHT: #999999 3px solid;")
    txtstream.WriteLine("    PADDING-RIGHT: 6px;")
    txtstream.WriteLine("    PADDING-LEFT: 6px;")
    txtstream.WriteLine("    FONT-WEIGHT: Bold;")
    txtstream.WriteLine("    FONT-SIZE: 14px;")
    txtstream.WriteLine("    PADDING-BOTTOM: 6px;")
    txtstream.WriteLine("    COLOR: darkred;")
    txtstream.WriteLine("    LINE-HEIGHT: 14px;")
    txtstream.WriteLine("    PADDING-TOP: 6px;")
    txtstream.WriteLine("    BORDER-BOTTOM: #999 1px solid;")
    txtstream.WriteLine("    BACKGROUND-COLOR: #eeeeee;")
    txtstream.WriteLine("    FONT-FAMILY: font-family: Cambria, serif;")
    txtstream.WriteLine("    FONT-SIZE: 12px;")
    txtstream.WriteLine("    text-align: left;")
    txtstream.WriteLine("    white-Space: nowrap;")
    txtstream.WriteLine("}")
    txtstream.WriteLine(".th")
    txtstream.WriteLine("{")
    txtstream.WriteLine("    BORDER-RIGHT: #999999 2px solid;")
    txtstream.WriteLine("    PADDING-RIGHT: 6px;")
    txtstream.WriteLine("    PADDING-LEFT: 6px;")
    txtstream.WriteLine("    FONT-WEIGHT: Bold;")
    txtstream.WriteLine("    PADDING-BOTTOM: 6px;")
    txtstream.WriteLine("    COLOR: black;")
    txtstream.WriteLine("    PADDING-TOP: 6px;")
    txtstream.WriteLine("    BORDER-BOTTOM: #999 2px solid;")
    txtstream.WriteLine("    BACKGROUND-COLOR: #eeeeee;")
```

```
txtstream.WriteLine("    FONT-FAMILY: font-family: Cambria, serif;")
txtstream.WriteLine("    FONT-SIZE: 10px;")
txtstream.WriteLine("    text-align: right;")
txtstream.WriteLine("    white-Space: nowrap;")
txtstream.WriteLine("}")
txtstream.WriteLine("td")
txtstream.WriteLine("{")
txtstream.WriteLine("    BORDER-RIGHT: #999999 3px solid;")
txtstream.WriteLine("    PADDING-RIGHT: 6px;")
txtstream.WriteLine("    PADDING-LEFT: 6px;")
txtstream.WriteLine("    FONT-WEIGHT: Normal;")
txtstream.WriteLine("    PADDING-BOTTOM: 6px;")
txtstream.WriteLine("    COLOR: navy;")
txtstream.WriteLine("    LINE-HEIGHT: 14px;")
txtstream.WriteLine("    PADDING-TOP: 6px;")
txtstream.WriteLine("    BORDER-BOTTOM: #999 1px solid;")
txtstream.WriteLine("    BACKGROUND-COLOR: #eeeeee;")
txtstream.WriteLine("    FONT-FAMILY: font-family: Cambria, serif;")
txtstream.WriteLine("    FONT-SIZE: 12px;")
txtstream.WriteLine("    text-align: left;")
txtstream.WriteLine("    white-Space: nowrap;")
txtstream.WriteLine("}")
txtstream.WriteLine("div")
txtstream.WriteLine("{")
txtstream.WriteLine("    BORDER-RIGHT: #999999 3px solid;")
txtstream.WriteLine("    PADDING-RIGHT: 6px;")
txtstream.WriteLine("    PADDING-LEFT: 6px;")
txtstream.WriteLine("    FONT-WEIGHT: Normal;")
txtstream.WriteLine("    PADDING-BOTTOM: 6px;")
txtstream.WriteLine("    COLOR: white;")
txtstream.WriteLine("    PADDING-TOP: 6px;")
txtstream.WriteLine("    BORDER-BOTTOM: #999 1px solid;")
txtstream.WriteLine("    BACKGROUND-COLOR: navy;")
```

```
txtstream.WriteLine("   FONT-FAMILY: font-family: Cambria, serif;")
txtstream.WriteLine("   FONT-SIZE: 10px;")
txtstream.WriteLine("   text-align: left;")
txtstream.WriteLine("   white-Space: nowrap;")
txtstream.WriteLine("}")
txtstream.WriteLine("span")
txtstream.WriteLine("{")
txtstream.WriteLine("   BORDER-RIGHT: #999999 3px solid;")
txtstream.WriteLine("   PADDING-RIGHT: 3px;")
txtstream.WriteLine("   PADDING-LEFT: 3px;")
txtstream.WriteLine("   FONT-WEIGHT: Normal;")
txtstream.WriteLine("   PADDING-BOTTOM: 3px;")
txtstream.WriteLine("   COLOR: white;")
txtstream.WriteLine("   PADDING-TOP: 3px;")
txtstream.WriteLine("   BORDER-BOTTOM: #999 1px solid;")
txtstream.WriteLine("   BACKGROUND-COLOR: navy;")
txtstream.WriteLine("   FONT-FAMILY: font-family: Cambria, serif;")
txtstream.WriteLine("   FONT-SIZE: 10px;")
txtstream.WriteLine("   text-align: left;")
txtstream.WriteLine("   white-Space: nowrap;")
txtstream.WriteLine("   display: inline-block;")
txtstream.WriteLine("   width: 100%;")
txtstream.WriteLine("}")
txtstream.WriteLine("textarea")
txtstream.WriteLine("{")
txtstream.WriteLine("   BORDER-RIGHT: #999999 3px solid;")
txtstream.WriteLine("   PADDING-RIGHT: 3px;")
txtstream.WriteLine("   PADDING-LEFT: 3px;")
txtstream.WriteLine("   FONT-WEIGHT: Normal;")
txtstream.WriteLine("   PADDING-BOTTOM: 3px;")
txtstream.WriteLine("   COLOR: white;")
txtstream.WriteLine("   PADDING-TOP: 3px;")
txtstream.WriteLine("   BORDER-BOTTOM: #999 1px solid;")
```

```
txtstream.WriteLine("    BACKGROUND-COLOR: navy;")
txtstream.WriteLine("    FONT-FAMILY: font-family: Cambria, serif;")
txtstream.WriteLine("    FONT-SIZE: 10px;")
txtstream.WriteLine("    text-align: left;")
txtstream.WriteLine("    white-Space: nowrap;")
txtstream.WriteLine("    width: 100%;")
txtstream.WriteLine("}")
txtstream.WriteLine("select")
txtstream.WriteLine("{")
txtstream.WriteLine("    BORDER-RIGHT: #999999 3px solid;")
txtstream.WriteLine("    PADDING-RIGHT: 6px;")
txtstream.WriteLine("    PADDING-LEFT: 6px;")
txtstream.WriteLine("    FONT-WEIGHT: Normal;")
txtstream.WriteLine("    PADDING-BOTTOM: 6px;")
txtstream.WriteLine("    COLOR: white;")
txtstream.WriteLine("    PADDING-TOP: 6px;")
txtstream.WriteLine("    BORDER-BOTTOM: #999 1px solid;")
txtstream.WriteLine("    BACKGROUND-COLOR: navy;")
txtstream.WriteLine("    FONT-FAMILY: font-family: Cambria, serif;")
txtstream.WriteLine("    FONT-SIZE: 10px;")
txtstream.WriteLine("    text-align: left;")
txtstream.WriteLine("    white-Space: nowrap;")
txtstream.WriteLine("    width: 100%;")
txtstream.WriteLine("}")
txtstream.WriteLine("input")
txtstream.WriteLine("{")
txtstream.WriteLine("    BORDER-RIGHT: #999999 3px solid;")
txtstream.WriteLine("    PADDING-RIGHT: 3px;")
txtstream.WriteLine("    PADDING-LEFT: 3px;")
txtstream.WriteLine("    FONT-WEIGHT: Bold;")
txtstream.WriteLine("    PADDING-BOTTOM: 3px;")
txtstream.WriteLine("    COLOR: white;")
txtstream.WriteLine("    PADDING-TOP: 3px;")
```

```
txtstream.WriteLine("    BORDER-BOTTOM: #999 1px solid;")
txtstream.WriteLine("    BACKGROUND-COLOR: navy;")
txtstream.WriteLine("    FONT-FAMILY: font-family: Cambria, serif;")
txtstream.WriteLine("    FONT-SIZE: 12px;")
txtstream.WriteLine("    text-align: left;")
txtstream.WriteLine("    display: table-cell;")
txtstream.WriteLine("    white-Space: nowrap;")
txtstream.WriteLine("    width: 100%;")
txtstream.WriteLine("}")
txtstream.WriteLine("h1 {")
txtstream.WriteLine("color: antiquewhite;")
txtstream.WriteLine("text-shadow: 1px 1px 1px black;")
txtstream.WriteLine("padding: 3px;")
txtstream.WriteLine("text-align: center;")
txtstream.WriteLine("box-shadow: inset 2px 2px 5px rgba(0,0,0,0.5), inset -
2px -2px 5px rgba(255,255,255,0.5);")
txtstream.WriteLine("}")
txtstream.WriteLine("</style>")
```

www.ingramcontent.com/pod-product-compliance
Lightning Source LLC
Chambersburg PA
CBHW070848070326
40690CB00009B/1746